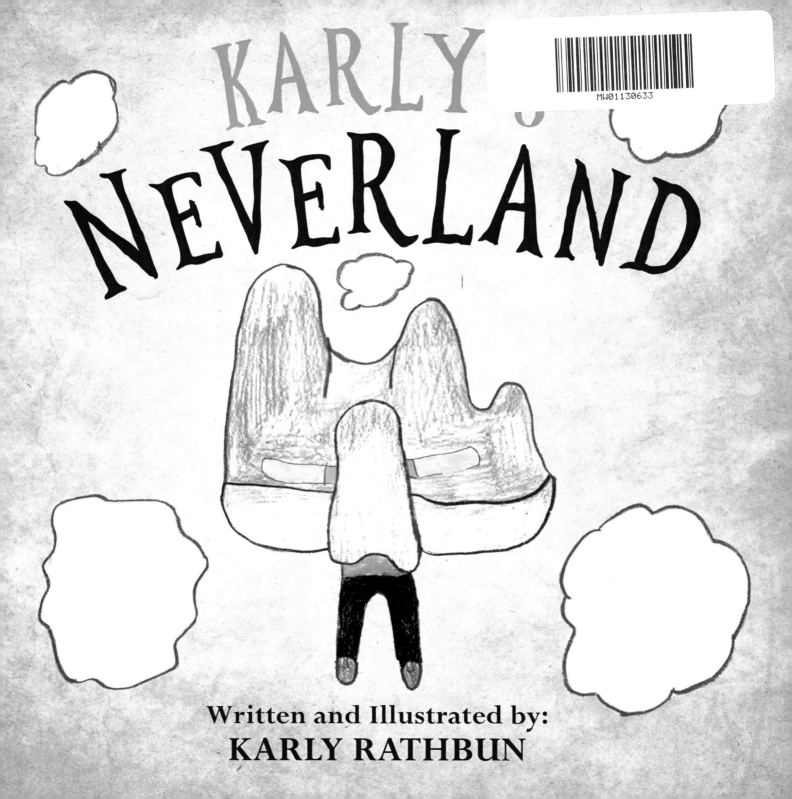

ISBN:
978-1-63308-588-6 (paperback)
978-1-63308-589-3 (ebook)

Interior and Cover Design by *R'tor John D. Maghuyop*
Illustrated by *Karly Rathbun*

CHALFANT ECKERT
PUBLISHING

1028 S Bishop Avenue, Dept. 178
Rolla, MO 65401

Printed in United States of America

KARLY'S
NEVERLAND

Written and Illustrated by:
KARLY RATHBUN

In Loving Memory
Trent David Ohlsson
March 8, 2004 – May 31, 2019

Trent was diagnosed with Ewings Sarcoma on May 29th, 2017. He had a deep passion for music and wanted to move to Atlanta, Georgia to become a music producer. Trent had a contagious smile and was always helping others out. He had the biggest heart and was my best friend.
I will forever miss him.

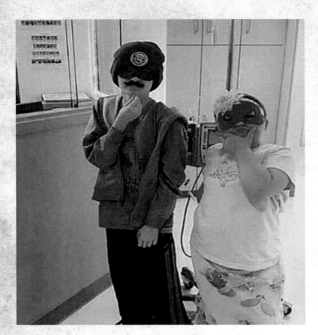

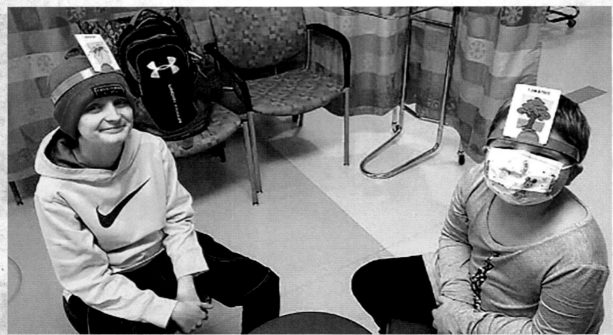

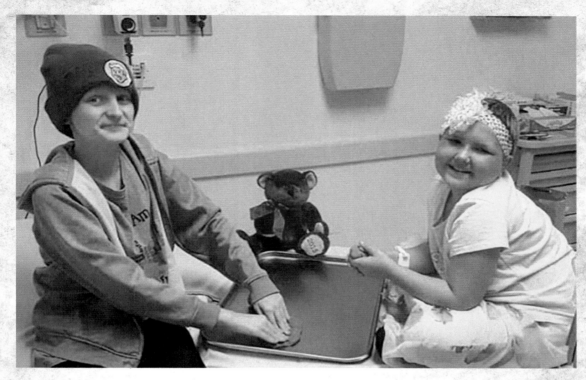

Thank You...

A HUGE thank you to all of my friends and family who not only has stuck by my side but has helped me win this fight.

To all my prayer warriors on my page, I love you all! To "Wendy" (Dr Ross), "Nana" (Allison), "The Fairies" (St Jude Nurses), "The Lost Boys" (all my battle buddies), and my "Peter Pan" (Trent).....thank you for giving me the best "weapons" possible for fighting off "Captain Hook" (Cancer).

Thank you St. Jude for being My Neverland. For being my safe haven and making sure Captain Hook stays away forever...... let's find that cure for cancer!!

Hi! My name is Karly.

Now on the outside I may look like your average 11-year-old girl, but on the inside, I have cancer. I was diagnosed with leukemia on September 18, 2017 and was sent to St. Jude Children's Hospital.

So grab a snack, sit back, and join my adventure on finding my Neverland.

Hospitals can be so scary. The one I was in had long, dark hallways, lots of weird sounds, and tons of people that I didn't know.

At first, I sat in a room and met doctors, nurses, and a child life specialist. This happened really fast and it was scary but that night I had a dream…

I was no longer in a room but soaring above the clouds. Down below is a beautiful island. I landed on the softest grass I've ever felt. I was surrounded by flowers, trees, and pretty, blue water.

I heard children laughing in the distance, so I went to look for them. On the other side of a valley I found lots of kids playing.

They were all different ages and looked all different, too. Some had no hair and some used sticks to walk. They looked like they were having such a good time.

I got up enough courage to say hi. They introduced themselves as Lost Boys.

We played together for what seemed like hours. Until a dog named Nana came to get me. She told me about a guy named Captain Hook that was out to get us.

He sounded so scary, but she said that it was going to be okay because I was in Neverland and the fairies would take good care of me. They were going to help me fight off Captain Hook. She said I would meet a doctor named Wendy and together we would win.

The fairies started to come around more and more. They brought weird things like crocodiles and pocket watches. They told me that Captain Hook was terrified of these things.

Only problem was is that those things also made me very sick. I lost my hair and also need sticks to walk.

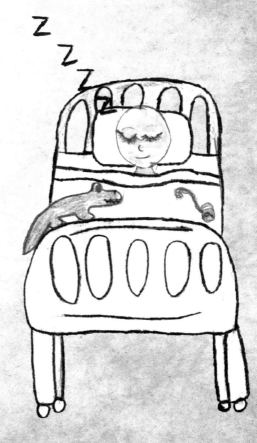

One day I was sitting by the stream and a boy with the softest voice said hi to me. He told me that his name was Peter Pan.

I knew from the start that he would be my best friend. We had so much in common! Anytime we had to fight off Captain Hook we did it together.

Peter Pan and I went on many adventures and were inseparable. Life in Neverland was good.

I learned the hard way that sometimes Captain Hook wins. I lost my Peter Pan on May 31, 2019.

And even though I know he's still helping me fight, Neverland just isn't the same.

I have been fighting off Captain Hook now for over two and a half years. I've met so many Lost Boys, became family with Wendy and the fairies, and continue to tell people about my Neverland.

On April 24, 2020, my fight will be won. I will ring the bell for all to hear! The Lost Boys and I will celebrate, and Captain Hook will be a thing in my past.

My dream ends with the Lost Boys no longer needing a Neverland. Someday I know it will happen, it just has to.

I DIDNT FIGHT ALONE

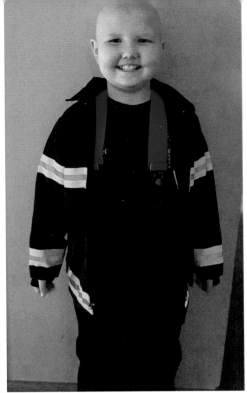

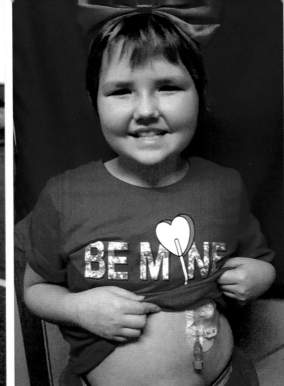
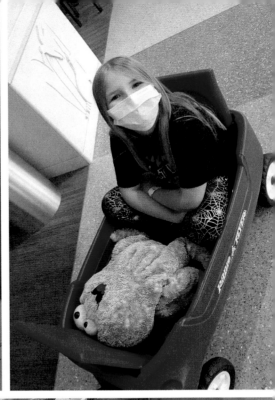

Team Karly!

Peoria to Memphis
ST. JUDE RIDES

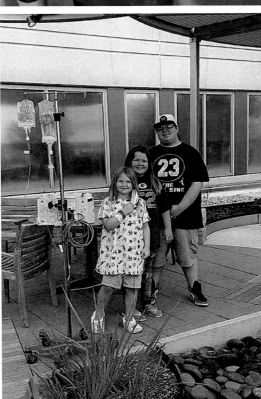

Made in the USA
Monee, IL
28 February 2023

28150018R00029